CW00866414

Marketing m
Questions and answers

Part 1

OTENG MONTSHITI

MARKETING MANAGEMENT
QUESTIONS AND ANSWERS
PART 1
Copyright ©2018
CONTACT ADDRESS: OTENG MONTSHITI
P O BOX M1139
KANYE
BOTSWANA

E-MAIL ADDRESS: otengmontshiti@gmail.com
Contact number: (+267) 74 644 954

Table of contents

Acknowledgements

Writing a book is not an easy task. Therefore I would like to thank our lord Jesus Christ, my family especially my lovely wife who supported.

Marketing Management

Questions and answers

Introduction

Champions are discovered during hard or trying times. Beyond every challenge there is promotion and breakthrough.

If you don't like them you will

never be celebrated in life and people who make it in life are always prepared for challenges.

Before people become presidents they prepare themselves outside parliament not inside.

Students must be prepared for examination. They must read their books and share knowledge and skills.

No man can exist in isolation. The following can help them;

1. Draft timetable

2. Conduct research because students who pass with highest grade read different books in that course.

3. Read a chapter and answer question on that chapter from previous examinations

this will prepare you for <u>NOTES</u> the environment of examination.

Students must trouble teachers by submitting assignment not vice verse because your future is in your hands and teachers are there to correct, teach and encourage you.

4. Form study groups

5. Identify your weakness and strengths. In examination begin with questions that you know you will pass with highest marks.

6. Mark your work before the examiners do the actual marking. There are no marks for quantity but what gain marks is quality

(accuracy, clear and well structured ideas).

W

7. Write as if the examiners don't know anything.

8. Be neat, correct spelling errors and avoid long sentences because they lose meaning.

1. Read your work atleast twice before you summit.

Key words in the examination

Explain- to tell somebody about something in a way that makes it easy to understand.

Mention/state/name/List- you write items one by one.

Discuss- to write about positive, negative and come up with

recommendations.

<u>Define-</u> you give the meaning of a word or phrase.

<u>Identify-</u> to recognize something and explain it in details.

<u>Compare/Contrast-</u>to differentiates between two things or more.

<u>Elaborate/ illustrate-</u> to explain something clearly and support your answer with diagrams or pictures.

<u>Distinguish-</u> to recognize the difference between two or more items.

NB Don't forget to give examples in the examination.

Answers

Follow instructions.

Use your own words as much as possible because examiners test your understanding and application.

Your answers must have:

Introduction

1. Should be short and specific.

2. It is used to explain key words or difficult words.

Body
1.. Should start with topic sentence which states the main point of the paragraph.

2. The rest of the

paragraph should expand or explain the topic sentence.

Conclusion

1. It states the writer's point of view or summaries the whole passage.

Summarize the main advantages and limitations of TWO methods of entering overseas markets used by marketing organizations. (1CM, May 2014)

International marketing is all about selling your goods and services to other countries. Some of the numerous modes or methods to enter these foreign markets are;

1. Licensing

2. Foreign direct investment/ green field

1. Licensing

This is the process whereby a company known as licensor gives its license to another company (licensee) at a fee.

The licensee trades using the licensor's trade marks, patents and processing methods.

Characteristics

1. Two parties should be involved namely licensee and licensor. The licensee applies for the license then the licensor comes and inspect the licensee's facilities. If the

2. licensee is approved by the licensor, he or she will be given permission to trade using their names.

3. The licensee is given permission to produce specific products. For example in Botswana Kgalagadi Breweries Limited has been given permission by Coca Cola to produce Coke products.

Advantages

1. The licensee is not going to market his or her products or services because the licensor is already a well known or established brand.
1. The products are not going to be viewed as outsiders because a local company is the one that sell the products or services.

1. The licensor will collect the fee at the end of specific period of time therefore the risk is in the hands of the licensee.

2. It requires less investment because the licensor does not need to establish any facilities but that issue lies with the licensee only.

3. The licensor's reputation will not be eroded because the licensee has to be monitored at all times using terms and conditions of their contractual agreement.

Disadvantages

1. When the licensor realizes that the licensee is making profits he may refuse to renew the contract.

2. When the licensee's products encounter bad publicity the licensee is likely to be affected.

3. As a licensor at the end of the contract the licensee is likely to become your competitor particularly if you are producing the same products.

Foreign direct investment/ Greenfield

This is the process whereby a company invests in a foreign soil (country). The company establishes a factory there (internationally). It may come in the form of buying shares. For example Motswana buying shares in a company in United Kingdom or United States of America.

Characteristics

1. The local government should be aware of what you are doing. Because most governments across the world detest companies selling drugs like cocaine, marijuana etc. and other harmful products.

2. There must be a
trade agreement
between two nations
(bilateral agreement).
For example Botswana
is an active member of
Southern Africa
Development
Community and
Southern African
Customs Union
therefore she has trade
agreements with other
member states.

3. There must be two parties or more involved from one country coming to invest in foreign soil.

Advantages

1. It creates good foreign relationship between nations. Countries around the world can live with one another in peace and harmony.

2. It leads to knowledge sharing. For example The Chinese are investing heavily in African to develop her. They share their valuable knowledge and skills with Africans.

3. The company will not be viewed as intruder rather as a local.

4. The company will come closer to its target market and easily learn their needs and wants.

Disadvantages

1. The company will face risks like change of governmental laws and regulations.

2. The local currency may lose it value.

3. Foreign companies may swallow up or consume local companies.

4. International companies come and dilute our cultural identities as local companies. Today people have changed dramatically in terms of behavior.

Highlight the benefits of sales forecasting and explain the advantages and limitations of TWO sales forecasting techniques you would use in a highly competitive market.

Sales forecasting is concerned with predicting future sales or demand. This is done systematically and different techniques are used in different situations or circumstances.

The following are the benefits of sales forecasting;

It helps the company to see the future of the company e.g. the future sales.

It helps the company in budgeting and resource allocation.

It helps to come up with strategies to overcome challenges in the future and how to tackle them.

It helps the company to know it weakness and how to convert them into strength.

The TWO sales forecasting techniques that I am going to write about are;

Trend analysis

In this method we look at the past or previous sales figures and then use them to predict or determine future sales.
It is assumed the same pattern will continue in the future.

For example; data collected over time or sales of the month of December.

Advantages

1. It is easy to do or conduct because you use the same pattern.

2. Past information is readily available from books of accounts like sales ledger and three column cash book.

Disadvantages

1. <u>ERRORS</u>-as the trend goes deeper into the future errors are

likely to occur.

2. It can be costly because it needs past papers which may not be available.

Management opinion

This is whereby you gather executives from various departments like Marketing, Production etc. and ask them to predict sales.

Advantages

1. It is easy because you just call executives from various departments and ask them to predict sales.

2. It does not need any expertise.

Disadvantages

1. Some executives may influence others like financial manager

may influence other because human resource manager 1. may feel he or she is an expert in that area.

2. Outcome may be biased because these people may not know anything about sales forecasting.

3. It is time consuming because of gathering executives which may

be a waste of time, **NOTES**
other valuable
resources and delay
decision making.

Write notes on three of the following:

a)   Public Relations

b) Brand image

c)   Integrated marketing

d) Merchandising

a) Public Relations

Public Relations is all about

creating a good reputation for the company and maintaining a good relationship with its publics. They include customers, suppliers, media, and so forth. It includes activities like:

Press visit

This is whereby you invite journalists to visit your facilities.

Free drinks and snacks are offered because if they are paid they will be viewed as propaganda.

Press conference

This is whereby you call journalists at a short notice after a major crisis or innovations e.g. During John and Johnson scandal when painkiller known as Tynol killed people.

A press conference was called by Jonson and Johnson executives to explain what really happened to rectify the error. The product was withdrawn from the market and people were refunded. Later it re-introduced it in very sealed package.

Johnson and Johnson used Public Relation strategies to win. It was Public Relation in

action indeed. Today it
is one of the most
powerful brands in the
world.

Press release

It is released by the
company to the editor
of a magazine or
newspaper.

It is used to announce
newsworthy articles
like new product.

It consists of the following:

- Sponsorship

- Customer relations

- Financial relations

- Government relations and many others

a) **Brand image**

It is the value that a specific brand carries in the mind of customers. Customers rank brands in their minds. In simple words, it is the picture that specific products and services occupy in the mind of customers.

For example if a customer want to buy a drink he or she is likely to buy Coke because it is powerful brand.

In 1985 Coca Cola introduced another coke which customers liked during their market research but Coca Cola was forced to remove it form the market because customers wanted the original thing or original Coke. In simple terms, they were emotionally attached to the original Coke.

Merchandising

It is all about how products are displayed in a shop It includes things like colors e.g. children like colorful layouts.

It is all about creating enough space between shelves in the shop so that customer can move freely.
It includes placing

convenience goods like sweets etc. at the point of sale to induce impulse buying.

Merchandising is deeper than that it involves stock rotation. This means older stock should get finished first before new stock. That is why products that are about to reach expiring dates are put in front of the new

product so that
customers may buy
them first.

Colder drinks are
always in front in the
fridge so that customer
can buy them first.

Explain the factors to be considered when setting prices for products and services.

Price is the amount of money or value a customer is required to pay to get an item.

In simple words it is the amount of money a customer is prepared to pay for a product or service.

There are factors to be considered when setting prices of goods and services. They are as follows;

Internal factors

Company objectives

Company costs

Quality

External factors

Competitors

Geographical pricing

Government laws

Internal factors

Company objectives

This is whereby a
company sets its
prices looking at what

it wants to achieve at the end of the day.

Some companies are profit oriented therefore they set prices to generate maximum profits.While other companies are there to cerate awareness e.g. some organizations exists to provide health issues to the community they operate in.

Company costs

This is whereby the company sets its prices looking at the costs it have incurred to produce those items. It includes all sorts of expenses like electricity, fuel, water and rent. Then we charge an extra amount or percentage as profit.

For example, if to produce a chair a carpenter needs nails, hammer, rafters and glue and they cost P500. Then he or she sells that chair at P750 his or her profit is P250.

Quality

This is whereby the company sets prices looking at the quality of its products and services. The higher the quality the higher the prices. For example BMW prices are high because their products are of higher quality.

External factors

These are factors which are outside the company.

Competitors

Here, the company pricing is determined by competition. In other words when setting prices we look at what the competitors are charging their customers.

When setting prices they should not be too lower or too higher than our competitors.

Our prices must be moderate.

In the market place there is price floor and price ceiling. Price floor is the minimum price you can charge your customers. If your prices are too low customers will start to question the quality of your products or services.

When the prices are too high customer will take business elsewhere.

Geographical pricing

The price tag of products and services are determined by the location of a business. If the company has a branch in town (Gaborone the capital city of Botswana) and another branch in the village the prices will be different in both locations.

Government laws

The companies should set prices looking at the laws in the country they operate in. government is the general overseer of every country in the world.

She must sure prices are favorable. This is done to avoid the situation whereby members of the public are overcharged.

There are times when the government can say a bag of onions should be bought at P50. This is very important to avoid price discrepancies.

Demand

If the demand of a specific product is very high the price is likely to be high.

What do you understand by the following words?

Direct costs

They are costs linked to the production of a specific product(s). There are two main direct costs namely;

Material costs include opening stock

This is the stock that

was left over at the end of the previous accounting year or period. Therefore it is the stock the business started with this year.

During the year the business may buy in new stock known as purchases and there is what is known as closing stock.

<u>Another indirect cost is labour</u>

This includes the hiring of workers who have directly concerned with the production of a specific product or service.

Indirect costs also known as overheads

They are general business expenses.

They apply virtually to

any business whereas the direct costs apply only to a particular business.

For example salaries, distribution costs, rental, energy costs, telecommunication bills, depreciation and so forth.

Explain the importance of the following elements to the marketing of fast moving consumer goods. (1CM,March 2012).

a) Packaging
b) Branding
c) Labelling

a) <u>Packaging</u>
Packaging is very important because it's

the first that encounters with a buyer or customer.

It is used for protection. If the product is well packaged it will not harm the customer is any way.

It is used in segmentation. For example kids like colorful colors while women like colors like pink, red and so forth.

It is used for storage purpose. For example, milk is packaged in such way that it will stay fresh as long it is not opened.

a) <u>Branding</u>

According to the American Marketing Association a brand is "a name, sign, symbol, or design or combination of them intended to identify the products or service of one seller or group of sellers and to differentiate them from those of competitors."

Branding is used to differentiate your products from your competitor's products.

Through branding customers can identify which brand satisfies that needs and wants.

It create value because **NOTES** customers will only take your seriously if your products are well branded.

b) <u>Labelling</u>

Labelling is usually part of packaging. It can be a well designed graphic or a mere tag. It contains information like the name of manufacturer, description of the contents, how it should be use or handle safely and so forth.

It is used to differentiate your products from the products of competitors. It makes it easy to identify the product(s) e.g. manufacturer, date of manufacturing, product name etc.

NOTES

Identify the stages of **<u>NOTES</u>** the product life cycle and summarize the key marketing activities associated with EACH stage. (1CM, Dec 2013)

Everything in this world has beginning and end. Products also have lifespan in the marketplace. They have introduction, growth, maturity, de-marketing and extension stages.

<u>Introduction stage</u>

<u>Product</u>

It is new product in the marketplace. It could be unique (niche marketing) or it could be for everyone.

<u>Promotion</u>

It is very high to show

customers where they can get the product through advertising.

Place

The product is made available in selected stores or individuals.

Price

The company can charge high prices to recover costs.

Sometime companies can charge lower prices to attract customers and then increase them at a later stage depending on the characteristics of the product (to increase market share).

Growth stage

Products

You add new features

like packaging and
benefits are added e.g.
discount, give some
items for free etc.

Place

You increase the
availability of products
on selected outlets and
distribution.

Price

It should be moderate

because people are now competing with you.

Maturity stages

It is more about maintaining the product in the marketplace.

Promotion

It is more of sales promotion but less of

advertising (to just remind customers about the availability of the product.

Place

It is now available everywhere.

Price

Geographical pricing— This is whereby the product is priced according to locations.

De-marketing

Product

Customers are no longer buying the product.

Promotion

There is no promotion at this stage.

Place

Unprofitable outlets are closed and remain only with profitable outlets.

Price

Clearance sale is common to clear the stock.

Extension stage

The company can decide to extend the life span of a product in the marketplace by adding new features and packaging e.g. Samsung 5 is an extension of previous versions.

Then repeat the stages.

Lightning Source UK Ltd.
Milton Keynes UK
UKHW021303210119
335934UK00012B/439/P